To Pat,
I saw this ... ...
of you" !
Happy Christmas 2001.
love Sandra.

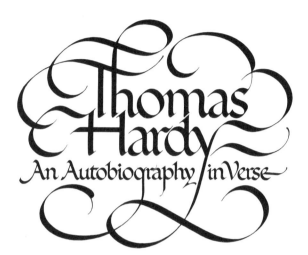

Thomas Hardy

An Autobiography in Verse

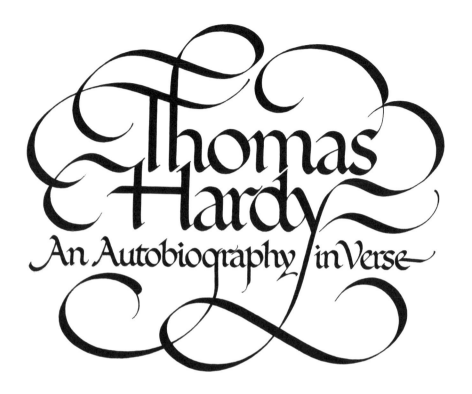

Thomas Hardy
An Autobiography in Verse

Eliane Wilson – Howard Shaw

Calligraphy & Illustrations
Frederick Marns

Shepheard–Walwyn · London

This edition © Shepheard-Walwyn (Publishers) Ltd, 1984

First published in this format 1984 by
Shepheard-Walwyn (Publishers) Ltd,
Suite 34, 26 Charing Cross Road,
London WC2H 0DH

ISBN 0 85683 073 9

Printed in Great Britain by Henry Ling Ltd, Dorchester,
on Harrow Matt paper made by St Regis International Ltd
and supplied by Eros Paper Company Ltd.

What is essential in poetry is firstly that it should be charged with emotion, and secondly that the moods of this emotion should have aesthetic or ethical value...

Thomas Hardy

to Anthony Werner

Acknowledgements

We are most grateful to all those who have helped us with this book: Dr. James Gibson for his generous advice and encouragement; Vera and Bill Jesty for their warm hospitality at Max Gate; Dr. Ray Evans, who guided us in and around Dorchester; Mrs. Jane Davis of The Old Rectory who looked after Frederick Marns; Mr. Joe Linee who gave of his time at Hardy's Cottage; the National Trust for permission to draw the Cottage at Higher Bockhampton; Mr. Robert Shield, Deputy Chapter Clerk, and Mr. Roy Spring, Clerk of Works at Salisbury Cathedral, who provided a key to the Close so that Frederick Marns was able to draw the cathedral at midnight. The text of the poems is taken from *The Complete Poems* (Macmillan), edited by Dr. James Gibson. The portrait of Thomas Hardy by Douglas Snowdon on page 137 is reproduced from *Thomas Hardy, O.M.* by Clive Holland (Herbert Jenkins Ltd); we were unable to trace the owner of the original.

Contents

List of Illustrations

Introduction

To choose Thomas Hardy as the first in our series of English Poets was relatively easy: much more difficult was the actual choice of poems and it was a daunting task to select a mere eighty from the nine hundred or so he wrote. Such a choice is by its very nature subjective and it becomes all the more so when one is dealing with a writer whose work is as intense, varied and personal as Hardy's.

Although Hardy has always been better known as a novelist than as a poet, it was as a poet that he wished to be remembered. For him poetry was the finest and most important of all forms of human expression, and he began writing verse as a boy and was still writing it shortly before he died. Most of his poems are undated; some were written in the 1860s, but the majority of them after he gave up novel writing in 1896. He often kept a poem and revised it over a period of many years. As a result it is almost impossible to arrange the poems in chronological order.

In this selection we accompany the poet at first through memories of his childhood steeped in the reminiscences and tales of the past recounted by his parents and grandmother; the links with Stinsford Church, his reluctance to grow old, the atmosphere of the home which meant so much to him and to which he returned throughout his life. Then come the poems of nature, memories of family and friends with the changes brought on — as Hardy saw it — by the tyranny and cruelty of Time, and some of his poems of early love. There follow the poems to his wife Emma, their 'deep division', the poignancy of Hardy's emotions after her death, and also poems about Florence, who was to become Hardy's second wife. Next come some war poems, and the collection ends with the reflective, elegiac poems of his old age.

Hardy's profound love of Dorset is expressed in the drawings of Frederick Marns. He has a special affinity with the poet in the precision, the acuteness and the quality with which he draws minute details. But in so doing, neither the poet, nor the artist, loses at any time the universal beauty of the overall picture. It is the perfect marriage of the particular and the universal.

'My art', wrote Thomas Hardy, 'is to intensify the expression of things ... so that the heart and inner meaning is made vividly visible'. No better words could explain the transcribing into calligraphy of Hardy's verse in this book — calligraphy, an art of total dedication where the artist, by the medium of his quill, increases and intensifies our consciousness of the written word through the beauty of his work, and the fusing of the arts of calligrapher and poet thus forges a closer link between the poet and his reader.

Hardy would surely have approved the lines written by an unknown scribe:

> Whence did the wondrous, mystic art arise
> Of painting speech and speaking to the eyes?
> That we by tracing magic lines are taught
> How to embody and to colour thought.

Eliane Wilson
Harrow on the Hill

Thomas Hardy

Thomas Hardy was born in 1840 at Higher Bockhampton in Dorset, a hamlet on the edge of the great stretch of heathland he was later to immortalise in his writing as Egdon Heath. He was not a strong child — at birth he was thrown aside as dead until the midwife noticed signs of life — and he grew up a solitary, introspective boy, aware of and moulded by the natural life around him. His powers of observation were acute and in these formative years his roots went deep; here on the heath and in the neighbouring valleys and woodland he daily met animals and birds and absorbed the rhythms of the countryside. Like most countrymen who live with its realities, he developed an unsentimental view of nature, yet early on he showed the capacity to identify with his fellow creatures, thus revealing the innate gentleness and compassion of his own personality. To the end of his life he remembered the death of a half-frozen fieldfare killed by his father with an idly-cast stone and he always opposed cruelty in any form. Above all, the unending cycle of the seasons, with their predictable moods and colours, together with the silence of the unchanging heath near his home, gave him the sense of timelessness that informs all his writing.

Hardy's father was a self-employed mason; his mother, a woman of strong character, had been in service. There were three younger children, a brother and two sisters, and for the first seventeen years of his life his paternal grandmother Mary lived in the same cottage. The household was secure and respected at a time when neither characteristic was to be taken lightly. Among Hardy's earliest memories were the tales told by his parents and grandmother round the cottage fire in the evening. The old lady remembered the heat of the summer during the French Revolution and told of Napoleon and the stir his doings had caused in a coastal area that feared invasion; his mother had a store of local memories, of folklore and legend, an oral tradition which Hardy's generation was one of the last to experience. Between them they created a world of romance and reality that an imaginative boy like Thomas would remember for years to come. Significantly, it was his grandmother's death in 1857 that led to one of his first poems, 'Domicilium', in which he recorded his grandmother's description of the family cottage in its earliest days.

The real world of nineteenth-century Dorset was not romantic. While some classes flourished — stone-masons among them — others did not. For the poor agricultural labourer life was hard and unrewarding, a mixture of toil, poverty and resentment. Shortly before Hardy's birth the trade union martyrs of nearby Tolpuddle were transported and Hardy himself knew of a shepherd boy who died of starvation. Of course, there was a bright side, even for the lowest, and the fairs, dances and local festivals that marked the rural year provided a measure of conviviality and relief. But the shadows were never far away. In the local town of Dorchester the Assizes took place, together with the public executions that sometimes followed. As a boy of sixteen Hardy witnessed from a favourable vantage point the hanging of one Elizabeth Martha Brown, an event that clearly had great significance for him and may be seen as one of the sources of inspiration for his novel *Tess of the d'Urbervilles.*

One of the first influences on the young Thomas Hardy was music. Both his grandfather and father had played in the instrumental choir of Stinsford church — indeed, as Hardy recalls in his poem 'A Church Romance', his mother fell in love with his father when she saw him playing in the gallery — and although the choir was disbanded when Thomas was a child, he soon learned the violin and, together with his father, was much in demand to play for dancing at local celebrations. Thus Hardy found himself part of a living rural culture, the folk music and oral poetry of the countryside. Not surprisingly, when he started to write poetry himself the folk idiom was much in evidence and he became a master of the use of refrain and repetition. He never lost his love of music and later on regularly attended concerts and the opera in London. His awareness of the consolatory power of music was explicit when he wrote of Michael Henchard in *The Mayor of Casterbridge*: 'If he could have summoned music to his aid, his existence might even now have been borne ...'

Jemima Hardy, whose own mother had married beneath her and who had known the shame of parish poor relief, was ambitious for her elder son and realized that the path to social preferment lay through education and hard work. She encouraged him to read widely and gave him books like Dryden's *Virgil*; she sent him to a nonconformist school in Dorchester where he learned Latin as a paid extra; and it is likely that it was his mother who saw an apprenticeship in the local office of John Hicks, an architect, as an advantageous opening for a bookish boy. Jemima was the major influence on Hardy for most of his life: under her guidance he became a voracious seeker of knowledge, filling notebooks with information wherever he went, and he developed a rigorous pattern of work that lasted into his old age; he was constantly aware of social rank and the problems faced by those who wanted to better themselves; and Jemima even seems to have been the source of his later philosophy that the world is ruled by an unthinking force indifferent to human pain and suffering: 'Mother's notion, and also mine,' he wrote, 'that a figure stands in our van with an arm uplifted, to knock us back from any pleasant prospect we indulge in as probable'.

Two friendships in these early years helped to move Hardy in a literary direction. The first was with William Barnes, a local poet who kept a school next door to the office where Hardy worked. A man of wide learning, though entirely self-taught, Barnes had a mastery of the Dorset dialect and must have given Hardy the confidence to use the same language in the mouths of his own characters when he started to write. It was Barnes who first resurrected the ancient name of Wessex which Hardy was to use to designate the area in which his works were set, and although he later met many of the leading poets of his time, Barnes was the only one to whom he was to acknowledge a direct debt. The other friend, more intimate and influential, was Horace Moule, the son of a local vicar, a brilliant but unstable scholar who recognised Hardy's promise and took him in hand, guiding his reading and introducing him to current religious and scientific thinking. Moule later committed suicide, thus contributing to Hardy's dark view of the workings of the universe.

In 1862, to further his career, Hardy went to London and joined the firm of Arthur Blomfield, a successful architect with a large ecclesiastical practice. For a sensitive young man it was a testing time and during his first years in London he experienced both elation and depression. He enjoyed the intellectual and musical life, going to the newly rebuilt opera house at Covent Garden, to art galleries and the theatre; but he was often lonely, he worked too hard and slept too little, and he was lacking in the social assurance that might have eased his path. In 1867 he was under such intense emotional and physical strain that he returned to the family home at Bockhampton, always his refuge in time of tension, and took up his old job in Dorchester.

Hardy was in many ways a secretive person and in his old age he burned many of his papers, so one can only speculate about the possible causes of this crisis. Partly it may have been that after five years in London he realized his chosen career was not one with long-term prospects. At the same time he had been writing poetry seriously, but all of it had been rejected, some magazines not even bothering to reply. For a man who once told a friend that he would never have written a word of prose if he could have earned a living as a poet, this must have been a harsh disappointment. Possibly more significant, however, was Hardy's loss of religious faith. He had always been a 'churchy' sort of person, as he himself put it, and until quite recently had seriously considered taking holy orders; yet by the time of his return to Dorset he had rejected Christianity. Again, the precise cause is not clear. It may have been his reading of progressive rationalists like Huxley, Darwin or Mill; it may have followed the breaking of a romantic attachment with Eliza Nichols, a girl to whom he had been more or less unofficially engaged for some time; or it may simply have been that his growing intellectual maturity had freed him from the unthinking religious beliefs of his childhood. Whatever the influence, Hardy not only lost his faith in a beneficent Christian God, he developed in its place the disillusioned anger against a Maker indifferent to the cruelties of his creation that was to become the constant theme of his writing. The poem 'Neutral Tones', marking the end of his relationship with Eliza and one of the most moving he wrote, comes from this period.

In 1870 Hardy was persuaded to go down to North Cornwall to survey the parish church of St. Juliot, which had long been in need of restoration. Here he met and fell in love with Emma Gifford, the sister-in-law of the rector. His later poetry, written in the remorse he felt after her death, casts an aura of romance over their first meetings amidst the wild coastal scenery, but there is no need to doubt the genuineness of their love. Emma's attraction for Hardy was her spontaneous gaiety, the sheer physical vitality that led her to shock the locals by riding her mare recklessly along the cliffs in the pouring rain, together with her real interest in literature; perhaps the fact that she had an uncle who was an honorary Canon of Worcester Cathedral confirmed her eligibility in Hardy's socially conscious eyes. For Emma, Hardy, with his London experience, represented the wider world and his laboriously acquired knowledge must have been impressive; more cynically one might add that at the age of thirty Emma must have seen him as something of a last chance to escape the intellectual wilderness of a remote Cornish village and set her cap accordingly. Whatever their mutual attraction in the initial phases of love, they were an ill-matched pair and in the long run their eventual marriage was to bring sadness to them both. This is not to say that they did not share any happiness. Clearly they did. They had several common interests: literature, foreign travel, animal welfare, in the 1890's the new rage of bicycling — Emma as enthusiastic and wild on her machine as she had been on a horse — and, even when the rift between them was apparent to all, they continued to read aloud together, one of the bonds between them.

Before he left London Hardy had turned to writing prose. His first novel, *The Poor Man and the Lady*, was never published, but it earned constructive criticism from George Meredith and his next attempt, *Desperate Remedies*, lovingly copied out by Emma, appeared in print in 1871. Once launched, Hardy was as dedicated and industrious in his writing as he had been in his accumulation of knowledge. *Under the Greenwood Tree* followed, based on the doings of his father and grandfather in the Stinsford church choir, then *A Pair of Blue Eyes*, in which he drew on his recent Cornish experiences. This last was published as a serial in a magazine, a form in which all his subsequent novels first appeared. It was *Under the Greenwood Tree* that attracted the attention of Leslie Stephen, one of the leading men of letters of the age and father of Virginia Woolf. As editor of the *Cornhill Magazine* he offered its pages for Hardy's next novel. When the first chapters of *Far from the Madding Crowd* arrived, he accepted the whole serial and gave much valuable advice on the construction of subsequent chapters. With this success Hardy abandoned architecture and became a professional novelist. In 1874 he and Emma were at last married.

For the next ten years Hardy and his wife had no settled home and they moved between a succession of rented rooms and houses in

London and Dorset. Of these the happiest times were spent in a house at Sturminster Newton. Here in the Blackmore Vale, overlooking the meandering Stour and its watermeadows, with the prehistoric forts of Hod, Hambledon and Bulbarrow on the skyline, Hardy wrote most of *The Return of the Native*, the sombre work in which the heathland of his childhood became virtually the major character of the story. But the idyll did not last and when he and Emma moved again to London strains began to show in their marriage, partly perhaps because of their continuing childlessness, partly because of Emma's restless and constantly disappointed social ambitions. Other novels followed, notably *The Trumpet-Major* and *The Mayor of Casterbridge*, before Hardy finally bought land on the edge of Dorchester and built his own house, Max Gate, a mile or so from his birthplace. Although he continued to visit London regularly and to travel extensively abroad, Hardy the successful professional writer had settled near the source of his creative inspiration.

Established in his redbrick Victorian villa, Hardy wrote *The Woodlanders* and followed it with *Tess of the d'Urbervilles*, the masterpiece that carried him to fame and fortune and into the fashionable social circles in London which he affected to despise but which in reality meant so much to him. Finally, in 1895, he published *Jude the Obscure*, the tragedy which shocked widely disparate elements of the reading public. Edmund Gosse, usually one of his strongest supporters, told him to his face that it was the most indecent novel ever written; the Bishop of Wakefield declared he had thrown it on the fire and persuaded W.H. Smith's circulating library to withdraw it. The gloomy story, in which the hero eventually commits suicide, defeated by circumstances and his own sensual weaknesses, to some extent mirrored Hardy's own melancholy in the 1890s. The rift with his wife was now open, an estrangement reflected in Emma's condemnation of *Jude*. Whoever was primarily to blame — and there have been protagonists ready to take up the cudgels on both sides — it is clear that they were now bound in a relationship in which they gave little to each other. 'All romance ends at marriage,' Hardy had written prophetically in *Far from the Madding Crowd*; in *Jude* he referred to matrimony as a 'sordid contract, based on material convenience'.

Jude was Hardy's last novel; from now on he concentrated on the poetry he had always believed to be his true vocation. Part of this change was no doubt due to the critical reaction to *Jude*, but it is a mistake to overemphasize this. Clearly he was badly hurt — he was notably sensitive to any hostile criticism — but the simple fact is that he had written his novels to make money; in his own words he had 'made a sort of trade of it'. With the pressing financial need now gone, he was able to turn to what he had wanted to do all along. In 1898 his *Wessex Poems* was published, many of which were early poems dating from the 1860s, and by 1928, the year of his death, seven further collections had appeared. Although he now found no difficulty in getting his poetry published, it was always a source of disappointment to him that he was usually referred to as 'Hardy the novelist' rather than 'Hardy the poet'.

In spite of his reception in London society and friendship with several fashionable women, there was little to lift the pall from Hardy's spirits in the 1890s. The hostility to *Jude*, his marriage, a severe attack of rheumatism, and the death of his father in 1892 — all combined to deepen his conviction that life is fundamentally a tragic affair. Three of his finest poems, 'In Tenebris', 'The Dead Man Walking' and 'Wessex Heights', come from this period, indicating the secret currents beneath the surface of his emotional and intellectual life. Four lines of 'In Tenebris' sum up the bleak mood:

> Black is night's cope;
> But death will not appal
> One who, past doubtings all,
> Waits in unhope.

The end of the century did nothing to kindle hope. When the Boer War broke out in 1899, Hardy had no sympathy with the jingoistic attitude of many of his contemporaries and lamented the way supposedly civilized nations settled their differences by physical force. His poem 'Drummer Hodge' attacked the futility and waste of war, while 'The Darkling Thrush' was both a dirge for a dying age as well as an ominous overture to the one just beginning. In 1904 his mother died at the age of ninety and he seems to have felt a sad relief at her escape from an unfair world. Meanwhile he had embarked on his long-planned epic verse drama, *The Dynasts*. Thanks to his grandmother's tales in his youth, the Napoleonic Wars had always been to the forefront of his mind — early in his marriage he had exhausted Emma by dragging her to the battlefield of Waterloo — and *The Dynasts* was his attempt to portray that conflict as a manifestation of the universal drama in which mankind is the victim of the Immanent Will, the unconscious Force dominating humanity and its aspirations. Although some regard *The Dynasts* as his masterpiece — which is how Hardy wished it to be seen — it is an uneven work and has been accorded much damaging criticism. Fortunately Hardy's reputation as a major poet does not depend upon it.

Hardy was always susceptible to women, from the simple village girls of his youth to the literary ladies of his successful years. Some, like his cousin Tryphena Sparks, with whom he had been going out shortly before he met Emma, or Mrs Florence Henniker, to whom he was powerfully attracted in the 1890s, he knew well; others he admired longingly from a distance. In 1905 he met Florence Dugdale, a young schoolteacher whose background had something in common with his own and who contributed to the children's column of a local London newspaper. She was nearly forty years younger than Hardy, but a strong affection grew between them and while she helped him revise *The Dynasts* he did his best to forward her work by writing flattering recommendations to publishers. The exact nature of their relationship and what, if anything, Emma knew of it are open to question, but with the aid of friends Hardy concealed their growing closeness and they even managed to go on holiday together. Wanting to see even more of her, he eventually contrived a meeting between the two women and they got on so well together that Florence was soon a frequent and accepted visitor to Max Gate. For Hardy, who had for some time given the impression that he believed himself near to the end of his life, Florence brought rejuvenation. His poem 'After the Visit' gives some indication of his revived strength of feeling as well as his attitude to her presence in the house which had of recent years become so dreary to him.

Emma herself had been seriously, and painfully, ill for some time and in 1912 she died. Any assessment of her relationship with Hardy must necessarily be superficial for the outsider never sees more than a small part of a marriage, but the evidence suggests that they had both contributed to the tensions between them. Hardy's interest in other women, however distant, cannot have helped and it must have been hurtful to Emma that of the twenty-odd love poems of *Wessex Poems* only one was addressed to her; furthermore, as her husband developed his taste for patronising other ladies with literary ambitions of their own, Emma found herself increasingly excluded from acting as his literary helpmeet, a rôle she had performed with great conscientiousness in the early days. As a firm Christian — indeed, a militant Protestant who abhorred Catholicism — she was genuinely shocked by Hardy's agnosticism and the attitude to marriage he showed in *Jude the Obscure*.

For his part, Hardy resented the superior attitude Emma adopted to his humble background and he no doubt found her narrow religious prejudices a strain; likewise, while Emma's childlike wildness may have been attractive when they were courting, her overdressing, inconsequential chatter and social pretensions must have been intensely wearing, and frequently embarrassing, in a middle-aged and elderly woman. Whatever the personal problems, however, it is difficult to avoid the conclusion that the dominant Jemima had much to do with the estrangement between husband and wife. Jemima and Emma never liked each other and the marriage had destroyed Jemima's dream for her children that they should not marry but live together in pairs. Certainly there was always a tension between Bockhampton and Max Gate and, surrounded as she was by members of the Hardy clan, Emma must often have felt a stranger in a foreign land. She retaliated by denigrating the family's social origins and bitterly resenting what she took to be, often wrongly, Thomas's failure to value her wifely devotion. Florence Dugdale, who witnessed some of the quarrels in the final years, summed up the situation sensitively when she wrote: 'I am intensely sorry for her, sorry indeed for both'.

The sudden loss of his wife, for whom he clearly had a deep well of affection whatever the discord of their day to day living, had a remarkable effect on Hardy. He now produced some of his most moving and beautiful poetry — the 'Poems of 1912-13'*: they were at once an evocation of the magic they had shared in their early love in Cornwall and an expiation, an expression of remorse for the sad years for which he knew he must be partly responsible. His other love poems pale into insignificance before those inspired by Emma's death. At their head he

* published in *Satires of Circumstance* (1914)

wrote the Virgilian phrase *Veteris vestigia flammae* — 'Ashes of an old flame' — and in these poems he achieved a sustained depth of feeling he had never managed before. Ironically, in thus making amends to his old love he was creating pain for the new one: Florence Dugdale, who had received Hardy's poetic tributes over the past five years, now found herself swamped by the passionate outpourings for the dead Emma. Nevertheless, Thomas and Florence were married in 1914, Hardy hoping that 'the union of two rather melancholy temperaments may result in cheerfulness'.

There was little beyond Max Gate to make them cheerful. The outbreak of the Great War filled Hardy with horror, confirming his view of the helplessness of Man and leading to more poems. He showed his compassion by visiting German prisoners of war in Dorchester and the war took its personal toll when Frank George, a young man of the next generation of Hardys whom he had made his protégé and heir, was killed at Gallipoli. Only a few months later his sister Mary died and this was in many ways the deepest loss of his life. He and Mary had been close from their childhood and their companionship had not wavered through all the vicissitudes of his career. She was an integral part of those domestic ties which meant so much and he regarded their relationship as almost a spiritual marriage. Her death sparked off new poetry, reflecting the happiness of their young days at Bockhampton and the warmth they had always given each other.

As the war continued, there was no pause in Hardy's creative genius. He went on writing poetry, some of it among his most tender and tragic, conjuring up the voices of the past; although there were strains in his marriage with Florence — the shadow of Emma stalked the rooms of Max Gate and Florence could make no changes to the house or garden — there are signs that he was aware of her needs more than he had been of Emma's and when he published his *Moments of Vision* in 1917 he gave her the first copy he received with the inscription 'to the first of women Florence Hardy'.

The final years of Hardy's life were loaded with recognition and honour. In 1910 the Order of Merit was conferred upon him; honorary doctorates came from Oxford and Cambridge; and many of the writers of the 1920s, among them Siegfried Sassoon, Edmund Blunden, Virginia Woolf, Robert Graves and Walter de la Mare, visited him, his sense of disillusionment striking a sympathetic chord with a generation made cynical by the Great War. He continued to work, almost up to his death. Meticulous proof correction and revision of existing books; new poetry collections — *Late Lyrics and Earlier, Human Shows* and *Winter Words* all appeared in the 1920s, the last named posthumously — each containing new poems as well as old ones revived; and more writing of his secret autobiography, the 'Life' eventually to be published as Florence's but which was, largely, Hardy's own work, his attempt to provide posterity with an authoritative biography tailored to his own wishes: to the end he maintained the disciplined approach that had marked his writing from the beginning. In 1920 he told a visitor: 'In writing, as in all work, there is only one way — *to stick to it'*. It could have been a motto for life instilled by the long-dead Jemima.

As late as the winter of 1926-7 Hardy could still walk over to Stinsford and beside the River Frome, the area of the Wessex countryside that had always meant the most to him. He died on 11 January, 1928, leaving instructions that he be buried at Stinsford with his parents, Emma and Mary. By one of those ironic twists that he might have appreciated, his last wishes were flouted. To satisfy those friends who wanted to ensure national reverence, his body was cremated and the ashes were buried in Westminster Abbey; as a gruesome compromise, his heart was removed and buried at Stinsford.

Hardy remains in many ways an enigma. If we read his character aright through the smokescreen he himself created, he was a man full of contradictions. Compassionate and tender to all living kind — he objected to the pruning of trees for fear of wounding them — he nevertheless could be insensitive to individuals and unforgiving to those who offended him; firm in his rejection of dogmatic Christianity, he never lost his love of the rituals of the church, its music and architecture, and at the age of 65 he bicycled some seventeen miles to read the lesson in church for a friend who was rector of Turnworth; much of his writing was determinedly tragic, yet he was irritated when charged with pessimism and up to a point he *enjoyed* his melancholy; rooted in the Wessex countryside, he revelled in the London season and travelled widely; he loved women — even in his eighties he deeply hurt Florence by his infatuation with the actress playing in a stage production of *Tess* — but his most memorable poetry was written about them when the individuals concerned were dead : it is a complex picture. What one can say is that he who studies Hardy's poetry will come nearest to the essence of the man; he himself once remarked that his autobiography could be found in his poems.

This is no place for a critical assessment of Hardy's poetry, but one or two comments may help the reader. First, in spite of the pervasive fatalism, Hardy is not primarily a philosophical poet. He said : 'I hold that the mission of poetry is to record impressions, not convictions' and it may well be that the least successful of his works are those in which his convictions are to the fore as, for example, in *The Dynasts*. Hardy's strength is in his power of observation, his ability to see the details of life that pass so many of us by. In a sense he wrote his own obituary in 'Afterwards', the poem in which he imagined the neighbours' comments after his death, when he wrote : 'He was a man who used to notice such things'. He saw nature with an unsurpassed clarity of vision, with the eyes of a sympathetic countryman who respects the mysteries of life and feels part of them; there is sentiment but not sentimentality. At the same time he had the ability to detach himself, to stand back and observe both himself and his fellow human beings in a wry, quizzical way; thus he was both observer and commentator, but never with prejudice or bigotry, always with the compassion and humility that recognises the common lot of mankind.

Hardy was one of the last English poets to be brought up in a preindustrial age. Rural Dorset was a remote place, agricultural and feudal, revolving in seasonal rhythms that had not altered for generations. Yet Hardy's lifetime saw many changes. It was a disturbing age, an age of transition in which the old communities were crumbling, the old certainties, good and bad, giving ground in the face of technological and social change. The railway had penetrated the Frome Valley before he was eight; horse-drills and steam threshing machines appeared in the fields as he grew up; social mobility increased as countrymen were pushed or attracted to the towns. Hardy was too much of a progressive — his politics were Liberal — to believe that this historical process was necessarily bad; but he had a powerful nostalgia for the past and he regretted the loss of the close relationship between man and the land. In a way he himself exemplified the changes taking place and there is an obvious tension between his determined climb into London society and the pull of his Dorset family background. It is perhaps this clash between ancient and modern, rural and urban, that partly accounts for the difficulty in delineating his character.

Hardy was an individualistic poet. With his close links with folklore and ballads, an oral tradition stretching back to the Middle Ages, he held aloof from the mainstream of Victorian poetry. The world of poets like Tennyson, Browning and Arnold reflected a culture that was increasingly urban and middle class, increasingly 'literary', and hence removed from country life. Hardy, despite his pleasure in fashionable London, never lost his rural roots. He was fascinated by the seasons, the weather, by heredity and the family, the continuity of life and all the concerns of living near the earth. Honest, austere, sometimes clumsy, he was prepared to write about anything that caught his attention, from the tragic ironies of daily existence to fly-blown pictures in railway waiting-rooms. In the end it is the simplicity, the unpretentious integrity of his poetry that enables him to transcend his age and speak to any generation.

Howard Shaw
Harrow on the Hill

The Poems

Let Me Enjoy

LET me enjoy the earth no less
Because the all-enacting Might
That fashioned forth its loveliness
Had other aims than my delight.

About my path there flits a Fair,
Who throws me not a word or sign;
I'll charm me with her ignoring air,
And laud the lips not meant for mine.

From manuscripts of moving song
Inspired by scenes and dreams unknown
I'll pour out raptures that belong
To others, as they were my own.

And some day hence, toward Paradise
And all its blest—if such should be—
I will lift glad, afar-off eyes,
Though it contain no place for me.

Domicilium

IT faces west, and round the back and sides
High beeches, bending, hang a veil of boughs,
And sweep against the roof. Wild honeysucks
Climb on the walls, and seem to sprout a wish
(If we may fancy wish of trees and plants)
To overtop the apple-trees hard by.

Red roses, lilac, variegated box
Are there in plenty, and such hardy flowers
As flourish best untrained. Adjoining these
Are herbs and esculents; and farther still
A field; then cottages with trees, and last
The distant hills and sky.

Behind, the scene is wilder. Heath and furze
Are everything that seems to grow and thrive
Upon the uneven ground. A stunted thorn
Stands here and there, indeed; and from a pit
An oak uprises, springing from a seed
Dropped by some bird a hundred years ago.

In days bygone—
Long gone—my father's mother, who is now
Blest with the blest, would take me out to walk.
At such a time I once inquired of her
How looked the spot when first she settled here.
The answer I remember: 'Fifty years
Have passed since then, my child, and change has marked
The face of all things. Yonder garden-plots
And orchards were uncultivated slopes
O'ergrown with bramble bushes, furze and thorn:
That road a narrow path shut in by ferns,
Which, almost trees, obscured the passer—by.

Our house stood quite alone, and those tall firs
And beeches were not planted. Snakes and efts
Swarmed in the summer days, and nightly bats
Would fly about our bedrooms. Heathcroppers
Lived on the hills, and were our only friends;
So wild it was when first we settled here.'

One We Knew

SHE told how they used to form for the country dances—
    'The Triumph', 'The New-rigged Ship'—
To the light of the guttering wax in the panelled manses,
    And in cots to the blink of a dip.

She spoke of the wild 'poussetting' and 'allemanding'
    On carpet, on oak, and on sod;
And the two long rows of ladies and gentlemen standing,
    And the figures the couples trod.

She showed us the spot where the maypole was yearly planted,
    And where the bandsmen stood
While breeched and kerchiefed partners whirled, and panted
    To choose each other for good.

She told of that far-back day when they learnt astounded
    Of the death of the King of France:
Of the Terror; and then of Bonaparte's unbounded
    Ambition and arrogance.

Of how his threats woke warlike preparations
  Along the southern strand,
And how each night brought tremors and trepidations
  Lest morning should see him land.

She said she had often heard the gibbet creaking
  As it swayed in the lightning flash,
Had caught from the neighbouring town a small child's shrieking
  At the cart-tail under the lash...

With cap-framed face and long gaze into the embers—
  We seated around her knees—
She would dwell on such dead themes, not as one who remembers,
  But rather as one who sees.

She seemed one left behind of a band gone distant
  So far that no tongue could hail:
Past things retold were to her as things existent,
  Things present but as a tale.

(M.H. 1772–1857)

The Choirmasters Burial

HE often would ask us
That, when he died,
After playing so many
To their last rest,
If out of us any
Should here abide,
And it would not task us,
We would with our lutes
Play over him
By his grave-brim
The psalm he liked best—
The one whose sense suits
'Mount Ephraim'—
And perhaps we should seem
To him, in Death's dream,
Like the seraphim.

As soon as I knew
That his spirit was gone
I thought this his due,
And spoke thereupon.
'I think', said the vicar,
'A read service quicker
Than viols out-of-doors
In these frosts and hoars.
That old-fashioned way
Requires a fine day,
And it seems to me
It had better not be'.

Hence, that afternoon,
Though never knew he
That his wish could not be,
To get through it faster
They buried the master
Without any tune.

But 'twas said that, when
At the dead of next night
The vicar looked out,
There struck on his ken
Thronged roundabout,
Where the frost was graying
The headstoned grass,
A band all in white
Like the saints in church-glass,
Singing and playing
The ancient stave
By the choirmaster's grave.

Such the tenor man told
When he had grown old.

A Church Romance

(Mellstock: circa 1835)

SHE turned in the high pew, until her sight
Swept the west gallery, and caught its row
Of music-men with viol, book, and bow
Against the sinking sad tower-window light.

She turned again; and in her pride's despite
One strenuous viol's inspirer seemed to throw
A message from his string to her below,
Which said: 'I claim thee as my own forthright!'

Thus their hearts' bond began, in due time signed.
And long years thence, when Age had scared Romance,
At some old attitude of his or glance
That gallery-scene would break upon her mind,
With him as minstrel, ardent, young, and trim,
Bowing 'New Sabbath' or 'Mount Ephraim'.

The Roman Road

THE Roman Road runs straight and bare
As the pale parting-line in hair
Across the heath. And thoughtful men
Contrast its days of Now and Then,
And delve, and measure, and compare;

Visioning on the vacant air
Helmed legionaries, who proudly rear
The Eagle, as they pace again
                    The Roman Road.

But no tall brass-helmed legionnaire
Haunts it for me. Uprises there
A mother's form upon my ken,
Guiding my infant steps, as when
We walked that ancient thoroughfare,
                    The Roman Road.

The Self-Unseeing

Here is the ancient floor,
  Footworn and hollowed and thin,
Here was the former door
  Where the dead feet walked in.

She sat here in her chair,
  Smiling into the fire;
He who played stood there,
  Bowing it higher and higher.

Childlike, I danced in a dream;
  Blessings emblazoned that day;
Everything glowed with a gleam;
  Yet we were looking away!

Childhood Among the Ferns

I sat one sprinkling day upon the lea,
Where tall-stemmed ferns spread out luxuriantly,
And nothing but those tall ferns sheltered me.

The rain gained strength, and damped each lopping frond,
Ran down their stalks beside me and beyond,
And shaped slow-creeping rivulets as I conned,

With pride, my spray-roofed house. And though anon
Some drops pierced its green rafters, I sat on,
Making pretence I was not rained upon.

The sun then burst, and brought forth a sweet breath
From the limp ferns as they dried underneath:
I said: 'I could live on here thus till death;'

And queried in the green rays as I sate:
'Why should I have to grow to man's estate,
And this afar-noised World perambulate?'

Midnight on the Great Western

IN the third-class seat sat the journeying boy,
　　And the roof-lamp's oily flame
Played down on his listless form and face,
Bewrapt past knowing to what he was going,
　　Or whence he came.

In the band of his hat the journeying boy
　　Had a ticket stuck; and a string
Around his neck bore the key of his box,
That twinkled gleams of the lamp's sad beams
　　Like a living thing.

What past can be yours, O journeying boy
　　Towards a world unknown,
Who calmly, as if uncurious quite
On all at stake, can undertake
　　This plunge alone?

Knows your soul a sphere, O journeying boy,
　　Our rude realms far above,
Whence with spacious vision you mark and mete
This region of sin that you find you in,
　　But are not of?

In a Waiting-Room

ON a morning sick as the day of doom
    With the drizzling gray
    Of an English May,
There were few in the railway waiting-room.
About its walls were framed and varnished
Pictures of liners, fly-blown, tarnished.
The table bore a Testament
For travellers' reading, if suchwise bent.

    I read it on and on,
And, thronging the Gospel of Saint John,
Were figures—additions, multiplications—
By some one scrawled, with sundry emendations;
    Not scoffingly designed,
    But with an absent mind,—
Plainly a bagman's counts of cost,
What he had profited, what lost;
And whilst I wondered if there could have been
    Any particle of a soul
    In that poor man at all,
    To cypher rates of wage
    Upon that printed page,
    There joined in the charmless scene

And stood over me and the scribbled book
(To lend the hour's mean hue
A smear of tragedy too)
A soldier and wife, with haggard look
Subdued to stone by strong endeavour;
And then I heard
From a casual word
They were parting as they believed for ever.

But next there came
Like the eastern flame
Of some high altar, children—a pair—
Who laughed at the fly-blown pictures there.
'Here are the lovely ships that we,
Mother, are by and by going to see!
When we get there it's most sure to be fine,
And the band will play, and the sun will shine!'

It rained on the skylight with a din
As we waited and still no train came in;
But the words of the child in the squalid room
Had spread a glory through the gloom.

On a Fine Morning

WHENCE comes Solace?– Not from seeing
What is doing, suffering, being,
Not from noting Life's conditions,
Nor from heeding Time's monitions;
  But in cleaving to the Dream,
  And in gazing at the gleam
  Whereby gray things golden seem.

Thus do I this heyday, holding
Shadows but as lights unfolding,
As no specious show this moment
With its iris-hued embowment;
  But as nothing other than
  Part of a benignant plan;
  Proof that earth was made for man.

February 1899

An August Midnight

A SHADED lamp and a waving blind,
And the beat of a clock from a distant floor:
On this scene enter—winged, horned, and spined—
A longlegs, a moth, and a dumbledore;
While mid my page there idly stands
A sleepy fly, that rubs its hands...

Thus meet we five, in this still place,
At this point of time, at this point in space.
—My guests besmear my new-penned line,
Or bang at the lamp and fall supine.
'God's humblest, they!' I muse. Yet why?
They know Earth-secrets that know not I.

Max Gate, 1899

44

The Year's Awakening

HOW do you know that the pilgrim track
Along the belting zodiac
Swept by the sun in his seeming rounds
Is traced by now to the Fishes' bounds
And into the Ram, when weeks of cloud
Have wrapt the sky in a clammy shroud,
And never as yet a tinct of spring
Has shown in the Earth's apparelling;
   O vespering bird, how do you know,
     How do you know?

How do you know, deep underground,
Hid in your bed from sight and sound,
Without a turn in temperature,
With weather life can scarce endure,
That light has won a fraction's strength,
And day put on some moments' length,
Whereof in merest rote will come,
Weeks hence, mild airs that do not numb;
   O crocus root, how do you know,
     How do you know?

Weathers

THIS IS the weather the cuckoo likes,
　　And so do I;
When showers betumble the chestnut spikes,
　　And nestlings fly:
And the little brown nightingale bills his best,
And they sit outside at 'The Travellers' Rest',
And maids come forth sprig-muslin drest,
And citizens dream of the south and west,
　　And so do I.

This is the weather the shepherd shuns,
　　And so do I;
When beeches drip in browns and duns,
　　And thresh, and ply;
And hill-hid tides throb, throe on throe,
And meadow rivulets overflow,
And drops on gate-bars hang in a row,
And rooks in families homeward go,
　　And so do I.

An Unkindly May

A SHEPHERD stands by a gate in a white smock-frock:
He holds the gate ajar, intently counting his flock.

The sour spring wind is blurting boisterous-wise,
And bears on it dirty clouds across the skies;
Plantation timbers creak like rusty cranes,
And pigeons and rooks, dishevelled by late rains,
Are like gaunt vultures, sodden and unkempt,
And song-birds do not end what they attempt:
The buds have tried to open, but quite failing
Have pinched themselves together in their quailing.
The sun frowns whitely in eye-trying flaps
Through passing cloud-holes, mimicking audible taps.
'Nature, you're not commendable to-day!'
I think. 'Better to-morrow!' she seems to say.

That shepherd still stands in that white smock-frock,
Unnoting all things save the counting his flock.

Shortening Days at the Homestead

THE first fire since the summer is lit, and is smoking into the room:
The sun-rays thread it through, like woof-lines in a loom.
Sparrows spurt from the hedge, whom misgivings appal
That winter did not leave last year for ever, after all.
Like shock-headed urchins, spiny-haired,
Stand pollard willows, their twigs just bared.

Who is this coming with pondering pace,
Black and ruddy, with white embossed,
His eyes being black, and ruddy his face,
And the marge of his hair like morning frost?
It's the cider-maker,
And appletree-shaker,
And behind him on wheels, in readiness,
His mill, and tubs, and vat, and press.

Great Things

SWEET cyder is a great thing,
A great thing to me,
Spinning down to Weymouth town
By Ridgway thirstily,
And maid and mistress summoning
Who tend the hostelry:
O cyder is a great thing,
A great thing to me!

The dance it is a great thing,
A great thing to me,
With candles lit and partners fit
For night-long revelry;
And going home when day-dawning
Peeps pale upon the lea:
O dancing is a great thing,
A great thing to me!

Love is, yea, a great thing,
A great thing to me,
When, having drawn across the lawn
In darkness silently,
A figure flits like one a-wing
Out from the nearest tree:
O love is, yes, a great thing,
A great thing to me!

Will these be always great things,
Great things to me?...
Let it befall that One will call,
'Soul, I have need of thee:'
What then? Joy-jaunts, impassioned flings,
Love, and its ecstasy,
Will always have been great things,
Great things to me!

Former Beauties

THESE market-dames, mid-aged, with lips thin-drawn,
  And tissues sere,
Are they the ones we loved in years agone,
  And courted here?

Are these the muslined pink young things to whom
  We vowed and swore
In nooks on summer Sundays by the Froom,
  Or Budmouth shore?

Do they remember those gay tunes we trod
  Clasped on the green;
Aye; trod till moonlight set on the beaten sod
  A satin sheen?

They must forget, forget! They cannot know
  What once they were,
Or memory would transfigure them, and show
  Them always fair.

51

Heredity

I AM the family face;
Flesh perishes, I live on,
Projecting trait and trace
Through time to times anon,
And leaping from place to place
Over oblivion.

The years-heired feature that can
In curve and voice and eye
Despise the human span
Of durance–that is I;
The eternal thing in man,
That heeds no call to die.

The Colour

(The following lines are partly original, partly
remembered from a Wessex folk-rhyme)

'WHAT shall I bring you?
Please will white do
Best for your wearing
    The long day through?'
'—White is for weddings,
Weddings, weddings,
White is for weddings,
    And that won't do.'

'What shall I bring you?
Please will red do
Best for your wearing
    The long day through?'
'—Red is for soldiers,
Soldiers, soldiers,
Red is for soldiers,
    And that won't do.'

'What shall I bring you?
Please will blue do
Best for your wearing
    The long day through?'

'—Blue is for sailors,
Sailors, sailors,
Blue is for sailors,
        And that won't do.'

'What shall I bring you?
Please will green do
Best for your wearing
        The long day through?'
'—Green is for mayings,
Mayings, mayings,
Green is for mayings
        And that won't do.'

'What shall I bring you
Then? Will black do
Best for your wearing
        The long day through?'
'—Black is for mourning,
Mourning, mourning,
Black is for mourning
        And black will do.'

Bereft

IN the black winter morning
No light will be struck near my eyes
While the clock in the stairway is warning
For five, when he used to rise.
Leave the door unbarred,
The clock unwound,
Make my lone bed hard—
Would 'twere underground!

When the summer dawns clearly,
And the appletree-tops seem alight,
Who will undraw the curtain and cheerly
Call out the morning is bright?

When I tarry at market
No form will cross Durnover Lea
In the gathering darkness, to hark at
Grey's Bridge for the pit-pat o' me.

When the supper crock's steaming,
And the time is the time of his tread,
I shall sit by the fire and wait dreaming
In a silence as of the dead.
Leave the door unbarred,
The clock unwound,
Make my lone bed hard—
Would 'twere underground!

1901

57

Molly Gone

NO more summer for Molly and me;
　There is snow on the tree,
And the blackbirds plump large as the rooks are, almost,
　And the water is hard
Where they used to dip bills at the dawn ere her figure was lost
　To these coasts, now my prison close-barred.

No more planting by Molly and me
　Where the beds used to be
Of sweet-william; no training the clambering rose
　By the framework of fir
Now bowering the pathway, whereon it swings gaily and blows
　As if calling commendment from her.

No more jauntings by Molly and me
　To the town by the sea,
Or along over Whitesheet to Wynyard's green Gap,
　Catching Montacute Crest
To the right against Sedgmoor, and Corton-Hill's far-distant cap
　And Pilsdon and Lewsdon to west.

No more singing by Molly to me
    In the evenings when she
Was in mood and in voice, and the candles were lit,
    And past the porch-quoin
The rays would spring out on the laurels; and dumbledores hit
    On the pane, as if wishing to join.

Where, then, is Molly, who's no more with me?
    —As I stand on this lea,
Thinking thus, there's a many-flamed star in the air,
    That tosses a sign
That her glance is regarding its face from her home, so that there
    Her eyes may have meetings with mine.

Regret Not Me

REGRET not me;
Beneath the sunny tree
I lie uncaring, slumbering peacefully.

Swift as the light
I flew my faery flight;
Ecstatically I moved, and feared no night.

I did not know
That heydays fade and go,
But deemed that what was would be always so.

I skipped at morn
Between the yellowing corn,
Thinking it good and glorious to be born.

I ran at eves
Among the piled-up sheaves,
Dreaming, 'I grieve not, therefore nothing grieves.'

Now soon will come
The apple, pear, and plum,
And hinds will sing, and autumn insects hum.

Again you will fare
To cider-makings rare,
And junketings; but I shall not be there.

Yet gaily sing
Until the pewter ring
Those songs we sang when we went gipsying

And lightly dance
Some triple-timed romance
In coupled figures, and forget mischance;

And mourn not me
Beneath the yellowing tree;
For I shall mind not, slumbering peacefully.

Old Furniture

I KNOW not how it may be with others
        Who sit amid relics of householdry
That date from the days of their mothers' mothers,
        But well I know how it is with me
                Continually.

I see the hands of the generations
        That owned each shiny familiar thing
In play on its knobs and indentations,
        And with its ancient fashioning
                Still dallying:

Hands behind hands, growing paler and paler,
        As in a mirror a candle-flame
Shows images of itself, each frailer
        As it recedes, though the eye may frame
                Its shape the same.

On the clock's dull dial a foggy finger,
        Moving to set the minutes right
With tentative touches that lift and linger
        In the wont of a moth on a summer night,
                Creeps to my sight.

On this old viol, too, fingers are dancing—
          As whilom—just over the strings by the nut,
The tip of a bow receding, advancing
          In airy quivers, as if it would cut
                    The plaintive gut.

And I see a face by that box for tinder,
          Glowing forth in fits from the dark,
And fading again, as the linten cinder
          Kindles to red at the flinty spark,
                    Or goes out stark.

Well, well. It is best to be up and doing,
          The world has no use for one to-day
Who eyes things thus—no aim pursuing!
          He should not continue in this stay,
                    But sink away.

Silences

THERE is the silence of a copse or croft
  When the wind sinks dumb,
    And of a belfry-loft
When the tenor after tolling stops its hum.

And there's the silence of a lonely pond
  Where a man was drowned,
    Nor nigh nor yond
A newt, frog, toad, to make the merest sound.

But the rapt silence of an empty house
  Where oneself was born,
    Dwelt, held carouse
With friends, is of all silences most forlorn!

Past are remembered songs and music-strains
          Once audible there:
          Roof, rafters, panes
Look absent-thoughted, tranced, or locked in prayer.

It seems no power on earth can waken it
          Or rouse its rooms,
          Or its past permit
The present to stir a torpor like a tomb's.

A Cathedral Façade at Midnight

ALONG the sculptures of the western wall
  I watched the moonlight creeping:
It moved as if it hardly moved at all,
  Inch by inch thinly peeping
Round on the pious figures of freestone, brought
And poised there when the Universe was wrought
To serve its centre, Earth, in mankind's thought.

The lunar look skimmed scantly toe, breast, arm,
  Then edged on slowly, slightly,
To shoulder, hand, face; till each austere form
  Was blanched its whole length brightly
Of prophet, king, queen, cardinal in state,
That dead men's tools had striven to simulate;
And the stiff images stood irradiate.

A frail moan from the martyred saints there set
  Mid others of the erection
Against the breeze, seemed sighings of regret
  At the ancient faith's rejection
Under the sure, unhasting, steady stress
Of Reason's movement, making meaningless
The coded creeds of old-time godliness.

The Oxen

CHRISTMAS EVE, and twelve of the clock.
'Now they are all on their knees,'
An elder said as we sat in a flock
By the embers in hearthside ease.

We pictured the meek mild creatures where
They dwelt in their strawy pen,
Nor did it occur to one of us there
To doubt they were kneeling then.

So fair a fancy few would weave
In these years! Yet, I feel,
If someone said on Christmas Eve,
'Come; see the oxen kneel

'In the lonely barton by yonder coomb
Our childhood used to know,'
I should go with him in the gloom,
Hoping it might be so.

1915

The House of Hospitalities

HERE we broached the Christmas barrel,
    Pushed up the charred log-ends;
Here we sang the Christmas carol,
    And called in friends.

Time has tired me since we met here
    When the folk now dead were young,
Since the viands were outset here
    And quaint songs sung.

And the worm has bored the viol
    That used to lead the tune,
Rust eaten out the dial
    That struck night's noon.

Now no Christmas brings in neighbours,
    And the New Year comes unlit;
Where we sang the mole now labours,
    And spiders knit.

Yet at midnight if here walking,
    When the moon sheets wall and tree,
I see forms of old time talking,
    Who smile on me.

In a Wood

PALE beech and pine so blue,
    Set in one clay,
Bough to bough cannot you
    Live out your day?
When the rains skim and skip,
Why mar sweet comradeship,
Blighting with poison-drip
    Neighbourly spray?

Heart-halt and spirit-lame,
    City-opprest,
Unto this wood I came
    As to a nest;
Dreaming that sylvan peace
Offered the harrowed ease—
Nature a soft release
    From men's unrest.

But, having entered in,
    Great growths and small
Show them to men akin—
    Combatants all!

Sycamore shoulders oak,
Bines the slim sapling yoke,
Ivy-spun halters choke
    Elms stout and tall.

Touches from ash, O wych,
    Sting you like scorn!
You, too, brave hollies, twitch
    Sidelong from thorn.
Even the rank poplars bear
Lothly a rival's air,
Cankering in black despair
    If overborne.

Since, then, no grace I find
    Taught me of trees,
Turn I back to my kind,
    Worthy as these.
There at least smiles abound,
There discourse trills around,
There, now and then, are found
    Life-loyalties.

1887:1896

On a Midsummer Eve

I IDLY cut a parsley stalk,
And blew therein towards the moon;
I had not thought what ghosts would walk
With shivering footsteps to my tune.

I went, and knelt, and scooped my hand
As if to drink, into the brook,
And a faint figure seemed to stand
Above me, with the bygone look.

I lipped rough rhymes of chance, not choice,
I thought not what my words might be;
There came into my ear a voice
That turned a tenderer verse for me.

Her Initials

UPON a poet's page I wrote
Of old two letters of her name;
Part seemed she of the effulgent thought
Whence that high singer's rapture came.
—When now I turn the leaf the same
Immortal light illumes the lay,
But from the letters of her name
The radiance has waned away!

1869

73

Neutral Tones

WE stood by a pond that winter day,
And the sun was white, as though chidden of God,
And a few leaves lay on the starving sod;
—They had fallen from an ash, and were gray.

Your eyes on me were as eyes that rove
Over tedious riddles of years ago;
And some words played between us to and fro
On which lost the more by our love.

The smile on your mouth was the deadest thing
Alive enough to have strength to die;
And a grin of bitterness swept thereby
Like an ominous bird a-wing....

Since then, keen lessons that love deceives,
And wrings with wrong, have shaped to me
Your face, and the God-curst sun, and a tree,
And a pond edged with grayish leaves.

1867

On a Heath

I COULD hear a gown-skirt rustling
 Before I could see her shape,
Rustling through the heather
 That wove the common's drape,
On that evening of dark weather
 When I hearkened, lips agape.

And the town-shine in the distance
 Did but baffle here the sight,
And then a voice flew forward:
 'Dear, is't you? I fear the night!'
And the herons flapped to norward
 In the firs upon my right.

There was another looming
 Whose life we did not see;
There was one stilly blooming
 Full nigh to where walked we;
There was a shade entombing
 All that was bright of me.

The Mound

FOR a moment pause:—
    Just here it was;
And through the thin thorn hedge, by the rays of the moon,
I can see the tree in the field, and beside it the mound—
Now sheeted with snow—whereon we sat that June
    When it was green and round,
And she crazed my mind by what she coolly told—
    The history of her undoing,
(As I saw it), but she called 'comradeship',
    That bred in her no rueing:
    And saying she'd not be bound
For life to one man, young, ripe-yeared, or old,
Left me—an innocent simpleton to her viewing;
For, though my accompt of years outscored her own,
    Hers had more hotly flown....
We never met again by this green mound,
To press as once so often lip on lip,
    And palter, and pause:—
    Yes; here it was!

Thoughts of Phena

At News of Her Death

NOT a line of her writing have I,
   Not a thread of her hair,
No mark of her late time as dame in her dwelling, whereby
   I may picture her there;
And in vain do I urge my unsight
   To conceive my lost prize
At her close, whom I knew when her dreams were upbrimming
      with light,
   And with laughter her eyes.

What scenes spread around her last days,
   Sad, shining, or dim?
Did her gifts and compassions enray and enarch her sweet way
   With an aureate nimb?
Or did life-light decline from her years,
   And mischances control
Her full day-star; unease, or regret, or forebodings, or fears
   Disennoble her soul?

78

Thus I do but the phantom retain
Of the maiden of yore
As my relic; yet haply the best of her—fined in my brain
It may be the more
That no line of her writing have I,
Nor a thread of her hair,
No mark of her late time as dame in her dwelling, whereby
I may picture her there.

March 1890

I Need Not Go

I NEED not go
Through sleet and snow
To where I know
She waits for me;
She will tarry me there
Till I find it fair,
And have time to spare
From company.

When I've overgot
The world somewhat,
When things cost not
Such stress and strain,
Is soon enough
By cypress sough
To tell my Love
I am come again.

And if some day,
When none cries nay,
I still delay
To seek her side,
(Though ample measure
Of fitting leisure
Await my pleasure)
She will not chide.

What-not upbraid me
That I delayed me,
Nor ask what stayed me
So long? Ah, no!—
New cares may claim me,
New loves inflame me,
She will not blame me,
But suffer it so.

A Thunderstorm in Town

(A Reminiscence: 1893)

SHE wore a new 'terra-cotta' dress,
And we stayed, because of the pelting storm,
Within the hansom's dry recess,
Though the horse had stopped; yea, motionless
    We sat on, snug and warm.

Then the downpour ceased, to my sharp sad pain,
And the glass that had screened our forms before
Flew up, and out she sprang to her door:
I should have kissed her if the rain
    Had lasted a minute more.

A Broken Appointment

YOU did not come,
And marching Time drew on, and wore me numb.—
Yet less for loss of your dear presence there
Than that I thus found lacking in your make
That high compassion which can overbear
Reluctance for pure lovingkindness' sake
Grieved I, when, as the hope-hour stroked its sum,
You did not come.

You love not me,
And love alone can lend you loyalty;
—I know and knew it. But, unto the store
Of human deeds divine in all but name,
Was it not worth a little hour or more
To add yet this: Once you, a woman, came
To soothe a time-torn man; even though it be
You love not me?

When I Set Out for Lyonnesse

WHEN I set out for Lyonnesse,
    A hundred miles away,
    The rime was on the spray,
And starlight lit my lonesomeness
When I set out for Lyonnesse
    A hundred miles away.

What would bechance at Lyonnesse
    While I should sojourn there
    No prophet durst declare,
Nor did the wisest wizard guess
What would bechance at Lyonnesse
    While I should sojourn there.

When I came back from Lyonnesse
    With magic in my eyes,
    All marked with mute surmise
My radiance rare and fathomless,
When I came back from Lyonnesse
    With magic in my eyes!

1870

At Castle Boterel

As I drive to the junction of lane and highway,
    And the drizzle bedrenches the waggonette,
I look behind at the fading byway,
    And see on its slope, now glistening wet,
        Distinctly yet

Myself and a girlish form benighted
    In dry March weather. We climb the road
Beside a chaise. We had just alighted
    To ease the sturdy pony's load
        When he sighed and slowed.

What we did as we climbed, and what we talked of
    Matters not much, nor to what it led,—
Something that life will not be balked of
    Without rude reason till hope is dead,
        And feeling fled.

It filled but a minute. But was there ever
    A time of such quality, since or before,

In that hill's story? To one mind never,
　　　Though it has been climbed, foot-swift, foot-sore,
　　　　By thousands more.

Primaeval rocks form the road's steep border,
　　　And much have they faced there, first and last,
Of the transitory in Earth's long order;
　　　But what they record in colour and cast
　　　　Is—that we two passed.

And to me, though Time's unflinching rigour,
　　　In mindless rote, has ruled from sight
The substance now, one phantom figure
　　　Remains on the slope, as when that night
　　　　Saw us alight.

I look and see it there, shrinking, shrinking,
　　　I look back at it amid the rain
For the very last time; for my sand is sinking,
　　　And I shall traverse old love's domain
　　　　Never again.

March 1913

Lines

To a Movement in Mozart's E-Flat Symphony

SHOW me again the time
When in the Junetide's prime
We flew by meads and mountains northerly!—
Yea, to such freshness, fairness, fulness, fineness, freeness,
Love lures life on.

Show me again the day
When from the sandy bay
We looked together upon the pestered sea!—
Yea, to such surging, swaying, sighing, swelling, shrinking,
Love lures life on.

Show me again the hour
When by the pinnacled tower
We eyed each other and feared futurity!—
Yea, to such bodings, broodings, beatings, blanchings, blessings,
Love lures life on.

Show me again just this:
The moment of that kiss
Away from the prancing folk, by the strawberry-tree!—
Yea, to such rashness, ratheness, rareness, ripeness, richness,
Love lures life on.

Begun November 1898

Under the Waterfall

"WHENEVER I plunge my arm, like this,
In a basin of water, I never miss
The sweet sharp sense of a fugitive day
Fetched back from its thickening shroud of gray.
  Hence the only prime
  And real love-rhyme
  That I know by heart,
  And that leaves no smart,
Is the purl of a little valley fall
About three spans wide and two spans tall
Over a table of solid rock,
And into a scoop of the self-same block;
The purl of a runlet that never ceases
In stir of kingdoms, in wars, in peaces;
With a hollow boiling voice it speaks
And has spoken since hills were turfless peaks!

And why gives this the only prime
Idea to you of a real love-rhyme?
And why does plunging your arm in a bowl
Full of spring water, bring throbs to your soul?'

Well, under the fall, in a crease of the stone,
Though where precisely none ever has known,
Jammed darkly, nothing to show how prized,
And by now with its smoothness opalized,
                 Is a drinking-glass:
                 For, down that pass
                 My lover and I
                 Walked under a sky
Of blue with a leaf-wove awning of green,
In the burn of August, to paint the scene,
And we placed our basket of fruit and wine
By the runlet's rim, where we sat to dine;
And when we had drunk from the glass together,
Arched by the oak-copse from the weather,
I held the vessel to rinse in the fall,

Where it slipped, and sank, and was past recall,
Though we stooped and plumbed the little abyss
With long bared arms. There the glass still is.
And, as said, if I thrust my arm below
Cold water in basin or bowl, a throe
From the past awakens a sense of that time,
And the glass we used, and the cascade's rhyme.
The basin seems the pool, and its edge
The hard smooth face of the brook-side ledge,
And the leafy pattern of china-ware
The hanging plants that were bathing there.

'By night, by day, when it shines or lours,
There lies intact that chalice of ours,
And its presence adds to the rhyme of love
Persistently sung by the fall above.
No lip has touched it since his and mine
In turns therefrom sipped lovers' wine'.

The Change

OUT of the past there rises a week—
Who shall read the years O!—
Out of the past there rises a week
Enringed with a purple zone.
Out of the past there rises a week
When thoughts were strung too thick to speak,
And the magic of its lineaments remains with me alone.

In that week there was heard a singing—
Who shall spell the years, the years!—
In that week there was heard a singing,
And the white owl wondered why.
In that week, yea, a voice was ringing,
And forth from the casement were candles flinging
Radiance that fell on the deodar and lit up the path thereby.

Could that song have a mocking note?—
Who shall unroll the years O!—
Could that song have a mocking note
To the white owl's sense as it fell?
Could that song have a mocking note
As it trilled out warm from the singer's throat,
And who was the mocker and who the mocked when two
felt all was well?

In a tedious trampling crowd yet later—
Who shall bare the years, the years!—
In a tedious trampling crowd yet later,
When silvery singings were dumb;
In a crowd uncaring what time might fate her,
Mid murks of night I stood to await her,
And the twanging of iron wheels gave out the signal that
she was come.

She said with a travel-tired smile—
    Who shall lift the years O!—
She said with a travel-tired smile,
    Half scared by scene so strange;
She said, outworn by mile on mile,
    The blurred lamps wanning her face the while,
'O Love, I am here; I am with you!'...Ah, that there should
    have come a change!

O the doom by someone spoken—
    Who shall unseal the years, the years!—
O the doom that gave no token,
    When nothing of bale saw we:
O the doom by someone spoken,
O the heart by someone broken,
The heart whose sweet reverberances are all time leaves to me.

January–February 1913

Overlooking the River Stour

THE swallows flew in the curves of an eight
　　　Above the river-gleam
　　　　In the wet June's last beam:
Like little crossbows animate
The swallows flew in the curves of an eight
　　　Above the river-gleam.

Planing up shavings of crystal spray
　　　A moor-hen darted out
　　　　From the bank thereabout,
And through the stream-shine ripped his way;
Planing up shavings of crystal spray
　　　A moor-hen darted out.

Closed were the kingcups; and the mead
　　Dripped in monotonous green,
　　Though the day's morning sheen
Had shown it golden and honeybee'd;
Closed were the kingcups; and the mead
　　Dripped in monotonous green.

And never I turned my head, alack,
　　While these things met my gaze
　　Through the pane's drop-drenched glaze,
To see the more behind my back....
O never I turned, but let, alack,
　　These less things hold my gaze!

The Musical Box

LIFELONG to be
Seemed the fair colour of the time;
That there was standing shadowed near
A spirit who sang to the gentle chime
Of the self-struck notes, I did not hear,
I did not see.

Thus did it sing
To the mindless lyre that played indoors
As she came to listen for me without:
'O value what the nonce outpours—
This best of life–that shines about
Your welcoming!'

I had slowed along
After the torrid hours were done,
Though still the posts and walls and road
Flung back their sense of the hot-faced sun,
And had walked by Stourside Mill, where broad
Stream-lilies throng.

And I descried
The dusky house that stood apart,
And her, white-muslined, waiting there
In the porch with high-expectant heart,
While still the thin mechanic air
Went on inside.

At whiles would flit
Swart bats, whose wings, be-webbed and tanned,
Whirred like the wheels of ancient clocks:
She laughed a hailing as she scanned
Me in the gloom, the tuneful box
Intoning it.

Lifelong to be
I thought it. That there watched hard by
A spirit who sang to the indoor tune,
'O make the most of what is nigh!'
I did not hear in my dull soul-swoon—
I did not see.

The Rift

'TWAS just at gnat and cobweb-time,
When yellow begins to show in the leaf,
That your old gamut changed its chime
From those true tones-of span so brief!—
That met by beats of joy, of grief,
      As rhyme meets rhyme.

So sank I from my high sublime!
We faced but chancewise after that,
And never I knew or guessed my crime...
Yes; 'twas the date-or nigh thereat—
Of the yellowing leaf; at moth and gnat
      And cobweb—time.

The Division

.

RAIN on the windows, creaking doors,
  With blasts that besom the green,
And I am here, and you are there,
  And a hundred miles between!

O were it but the weather, Dear,
  O were it but the miles
That summed up all our severance,
  There might be room for smiles.

But that thwart thing betwixt us twain,
  Which nothing cleaves or clears,
Is more than distance, Dear, or rain,
  And longer than the years!

1893

In Tenebris 1

WINTERTIME nighs;
But my bereavement-pain
It cannot bring again:
Twice no one dies.

Flower-petals flee;
But, since it once hath been,
No more that severing scene
Can harrow me.

Birds faint in dread:
I shall not lose old strength
In the lone frost's black length:
Strength long since fled!

Leaves freeze to dun;
But friends can not turn cold
This season as of old
For him with none.

Tempests may scath;
But love can not make smart
Again this year his heart
Who no heart hath.

Black is night's cope;
But death will not appal
One who, past doubting's all,
Waits in unhope.

The Dead Man Walking

THEY hail me as one living,
    But don't they know
That I have died of late years,
    Untombed although?

I am but a shape that stands here,
    A pulseless mould,
A pale past picture, screening
    Ashes gone cold.

Not at a minute's warning,
    Not in a loud hour,
For me ceased Time's enchantments
    In hall and bower.

There was no tragic transit,
    No catch of breath,
When silent seasons inched me
    On to this death....

—A Troubadour-youth I rambled
    With Life for lyre,
The beats of being raging
    In me like fire.

But when I practised eyeing
    The goal of men,
It iced me, and I perished
    A little then.

When passed my friend, my kinsfolk,
    Through the Last Door,
And left me standing bleakly,
    I died yet more;

And when my Love's heart kindled
    In hate of me,
Wherefore I knew not, died I
    One more degree.

And if when I died fully,
I cannot say,
And changed into the corpse-thing
I am to-day;

Yet is it that, though whiling
The time somehow
In walking, talking, smiling,
I live not now.

Wessex Heights

THERE are some heights in Wessex, shaped as if by a kindly hand
For thinking, dreaming, dying on, and at crises when I stand,
Say, on Ingpen Beacon eastward, or on Wylls-Neck westwardly,
I seem where I was before my birth, and after death may be.

In the lowlands I have no comrade, not even the lone man's friend—
Her who suffereth long and is kind; accepts what he is too weak to
      mend:
Down there they are dubious and askance; there nobody thinks as I,
But mind-chains do not clank where one's next neighbour is the sky.

In the towns I am tracked by phantoms having weird detective ways—
Shadows of beings who fellowed with myself of earlier days:
They hang about at places, and they say harsh heavy things—
Men with a wintry sneer, and women with tart disparagings.

Down there I seem to be false to myself, my simple self that was,
And is not now, and I see him watching, wondering what crass cause
Can have merged him into such a strange continuator as this,
Who yet has something in common with himself, my chrysalis.

I cannot go to the great grey Plain; there's a figure against the moon,
Nobody sees it but I, and it makes my breast beat out of tune;
I cannot go to the tall-spired town, being barred by the forms now passed
For everybody but me, in whose long vision they stand there fast.

There's a ghost at Yell'ham Bottom chiding loud at the fall of the night,
There's a ghost in Froom-side Vale, thin-lipped and vague, in a shroud of white,
There is one in the railway train whenever I do not want it near;
I see its profile against the pane, saying what I would not hear.

As for one rare fair woman, I am now but a thought of hers,
I enter her mind and another thought succeeds me that she prefers;
Yet my love for her in its fulness she herself even did not know;
Well, time cures hearts of tenderness, and now I can let her go.

So I am found on Ingpen Beacon, or on Wylls-Neck to the west,
Or else on homely Bulbarrow, or little Pilsdon Crest,
Where men have never cared to haunt, nor women have walked
            with me,
And ghosts then keep their distance; and I know some liberty.

1896

The Darkling Thrush

I LEANT upon a coppice gate
 When frost was spectre-gray,
And Winter's dregs made desolate
 The weakening eye of day.
The tangled bine-stems scored the sky
 Like strings of broken lyres,
And all mankind that haunted nigh
 Had sought their household fires.

The land's sharp features seemed to be
 The Century's corpse outleant,
His crypt the cloudy canopy,
 The wind his death-lament.
The ancient pulse of germ and birth
 Was shrunken hard and dry,
And every spirit upon earth
 Seemed fervourless as I.

At once a voice arose among
    The bleak twigs overhead
In a full-hearted evensong
    Of joy illimited;
An aged thrush, frail, gaunt, and small,
    In blast-beruffled plume,
Had chosen thus to fling his soul
    Upon the growing gloom.

So little cause for carolings
    Of such ecstatic sound
Was written on terrestrial things
    Afar or nigh around,
That I could think there trembled through
    His happy good-night air
Some blessed Hope, whereof he knew
    And I was unaware.

31 December 1900

Wives in the Sere

NEVER a careworn wife but shows,
　　If a joy suffuse her,
Something beautiful to those
　　Patient to peruse her,
Some one charm the world unknows
　　Precious to a muser,
Haply what, ere years were foes,
　　Moved her mate to choose her.

But, be it a hint of rose
　　That an instant hues her,
Or some early light or pose
　　Wherewith thought renews her,
Seen by him at full, ere woes
　　Practised to abuse her,
Sparely comes it, swiftly goes,
　　Time again subdues her.

I Look Into My Glass

I LOOK into my glass,
And view my wasting skin,
And say, 'Would God it came to pass
My heart had shrunk as thin!'

For then, I, undistrest
By hearts grown cold to me,
Could lonely wait my endless rest
With equanimity.

But Time, to make me grieve,
Part steals, lets part abide;
And shakes this fragile frame at eve
With throbbings of noontide.

Lost Love

I PLAY my sweet old airs—
The airs he knew
When our love was true—
But he does not balk
His determined walk,
And passes up the stairs.

I sing my songs once more,
And presently hear
His footstep near
As if it would stay;
But he goes his way,
And shuts a distant door.

So I wait for another morn,
And another night
In this soul-sick blight;
And I wonder much
As I sit, why such
A woman as I was born!

Penance

'WHY do you sit, O pale thin man,
    At the end of the room
By that harpsichord, built on the quaint old plan?
    —It is cold as a tomb,
And there's not a spark within the grate;
    And the jingling wires
    Are as vain desires
    That have lagged too late.

Why do I? Alas, far times ago
    A woman lyred here
In the evenfall; one who fain did so
    From year to year;

And, in loneliness bending wistfully,
    Would wake each note
    In sick sad rote,
    None to listen or see!

'I would not join. I would not stay,
    But drew away,
Though the winter fire beamed brightly....Aye!
    I do to-day
What I would not then; and the chill old keys,
    Like a skull's brown teeth
    Loose in their sheath,
    Freeze my touch; yes, freeze!'

The Wound

I CLIMBED to the crest,
  And, fog-festooned,
The sun lay west
  Like a crimson wound:

Like that wound of mine
  Of which none knew,
For I'd given no sign
  That it pierced me through.

The Spell of the Rose

I MEAN to build a hall anon,
　　And shape two turrets there,
　　And a broad newelled stair,
And a cool well for crystal water;
　　Yes; I will build a hall anon,
　　Plant roses love shall feed upon,
　　And apple-trees and pear.

He set to build the manor-hall,
　　And shaped the turrets there,
　　And the broad newelled stair,
And the cool well for crystal water;
　　He built for me that manor-hall,
　　And planted many trees withal,
　　But no rose anywhere.

And as he planted never a rose
That bears the flower of love,
Though other flowers throve
Some heart-bane moved our souls to sever
Since he had planted never a rose;
And misconceits raised horrid shows,
And agonies came thereof.

'I'll mend these miseries,' then said I,
And so, at dead of night,
I went and, screened from sight,
That nought should keep our souls in severance,
I set a rose-bush. This,' said I,
'May end divisions dire and wry,
And long-drawn days of blight.'

But I was called from earth-yea, called
Before my rose-bush grew;
And would that now I knew
What feels he of the tree I planted,
And whether, after I was called
To be a ghost, he, as of old,
Gave me his heart anew!

Perhaps now blooms that queen of trees
I set but saw not grow,
And he, beside its glow—
Eyes couched of the mis-vision that blurred me—
Ay, there beside that queen of trees
He sees me as I was, though sees
Too late to tell me so!

The Going

WHY did you give no hint that night
That quickly after the morrow's dawn,
And calmly, as if indifferent quite,
You would close your term here, up and be gone
　　　Where I could not follow
　　　With wing of swallow
To gain one glimpse of you ever anon!

　　　Never to bid good-bye,
　　　Or lip me the softest call,
Or utter a wish for a word, while I
Saw morning harden upon the wall,
　　　Unmoved, unknowing
　　　That your great going
Had place that moment, and altered all.

Why do you make me leave the house
And think for a breath it is you I see
At the end of the alley of bending boughs
Where so often at dusk you used to be;
    Till in darkening dankness
    The yawning blankness
Of the perspective sickens me!

    You were she who abode
    By those red-veined rocks far West,
You were the swan-necked one who rode
Along the beetling Beeny Crest,
    And, reining nigh me,
    Would muse and eye me,
While Life unrolled us its very best.

Why, then, latterly did we not speak,
Did we not think of those days long dead,
And ere your vanishing strive to seek
That time's renewal? We might have said,
        'In this bright spring weather
        We'll visit together
Those places that once we visited'.

        Well, well! All's past amend,
        Unchangeable. It must go.
I seem but a dead man held on end
To sink down soon.... O you could not know
        That such swift fleeing
        No soul foreseeing—
Not even I—would undo me so!

December 1912

Read by Moonlight

I PAUSED to read a letter of hers
   By the moon's cold shine,
Eyeing it in the tenderest way,
And edging it up to catch each ray
   Upon her light-penned line.
I did not know what years would flow
   Of her life's span and mine
Ere I read another letter of hers
   By the moon's cold shine!

I chance now on the last of hers,
   By the moon's cold shine;
It is the one remaining page
Out of the many shallow and sage
   Whereto she set her sign.
Who could foresee there were to be
   Such missives of pain and pine
Ere I should read this last of hers
   By the moon's cold shine!

An Upbraiding

NOW I am dead you sing to me
    The songs we used to know,
But while I lived you had no wish
    Or care for doing so.

Now I am dead you come to me
    In the moonlight, comfortless;
Ah, what would I have given alive
    To win such tenderness!

When you are dead, and stand to me
    Not differenced, as now,
But like again, will you be cold
    As when we lived, or how?

The Shadow on the Stone

I WENT by the Druid stone
That broods in the garden white and lone,
And I stopped and looked at the shifting shadows
That at some moments fall thereon
From the tree hard by with a rhythmic swing,
And they shaped in my imagining
To the shade that a well-known head and shoulders
Threw there when she was gardening.

I thought her behind my back,
Yea, her I long had learned to lack,
And I said: 'I am sure you are standing behind me,
Though how do you get into this old track?'
And there was no sound but the fall of a leaf
As a sad response; and to keep down grief
I would not turn my head to discover
That there was nothing in my belief.

Yet I wanted to look and see
That nobody stood at the back of me;
But I thought once more: 'Nay, I'll not unvision
A shape which, somehow, there may be.'
So I went on softly from the glade,
And left her behind me throwing her shade,
As she were indeed an apparition—
My head unturned lest my dream should fade.

Begun 1913 finished 1916

The Haunter

HE does not think that I haunt here nightly:
  How shall I let him know
That whither his fancy sets him wandering
  I, too, alertly go?—
Hover and hover a few feet from him
  Just as I used to do,
But cannot answer the words he lifts me—
  Only listen thereto!

When I could answer he did not say them:
  When I could let him know
How I would like to join in his journeys
  Seldom he wished to go.
Now that he goes and wants me with him
  More than he used to do,
Never he sees my faithful phantom
  Though he speaks thereto.

Yes, I companion him to places
Only dreamers know,
Where the shy hares print long paces,
Where the night rooks go;
Into old aisles where the past is all to him,
Close as his shade can do,
Always lacking the power to call to him,
Near as I reach thereto!

What a good haunter I am, O tell him!
Quickly make him know
If he but sigh since my loss befell him
Straight to his side I go.
Tell him a faithful one is doing
All that love can do
Still that his path may be worth pursuing,
And to bring peace thereto.

The Voice

WOMAN much missed, how you call to me, call to me,
Saying that now you are not as you were
When you had changed from the one who was all to me,
But as at first, when our day was fair.

Can it be you that I hear? Let me view you, then,
Standing as when I drew near to the town
Where you would wait for me: yes, as I knew you then,
Even to the original air-blue gown!

Or is it only the breeze, in its listlessness
Travelling across the wet mead to me here,
You being ever dissolved to wan wistlessness,
Heard no more again far or near?

Thus I; faltering forward,
Leaves around me falling,
Wind oozing thin through the thorn from norward,
And the woman calling.

December 1912

After a Journey

HERETO I come to view a voiceless ghost;
    Whither, O whither will its whim now draw me?
Up the cliff, down, till I'm lonely, lost,
    And the unseen waters' ejaculations awe me.
Where you will next be there's no knowing,
    Facing round about me everywhere,
      With your nut-coloured hair,
And gray eyes, and rose-flush coming and going.

Yes: I have re-entered your olden haunts at last;
    Through the years, through the dead scenes I have tracked you;
What have you now found to say of our past—
    Scanned across the dark space wherein I have lacked you?
Summer gave us sweets, but autumn wrought division?
    Things were not lastly as firstly well
      With us twain, you tell?
But all's closed now, despite Time's derision.

I see what you are doing: you are leading me on
    To the spots we knew when we haunted here together,
The waterfall, above which the mist-bow shone
    At the then fair hour in then fair weather,
And the cave just under, with a voice still so hollow
    That it seems to call out to me from forty years ago,
        When you were all aglow,
And not the thin ghost that I now frailly follow!

Ignorant of what there is flitting here to see,
    The waked birds preen and the seals flop lazily;
Soon you will have, Dear, to vanish from me,
    For the stars close their shutters and the dawn whitens hazily.
Trust me, I mind not, though Life lours,
    The bringing me here; nay, bring me here again!
        I am just the same as when
Our days were a joy, and our paths through flowers.

Pentargan Bay

A Night in November

I MARKED when the weather changed,
And the panes began to quake,
And the winds rose up and ranged,
That night, lying half-awake.

Dead leaves blew into my room,
And alighted upon my bed,
And a tree declared to the gloom
Its sorrow that they were shed.

One leaf of them touched my hand,
And I thought that it was you
There stood as you used to stand,
And saying at last you knew!

(?)1913

She Opened the Door

SHE opened the door of the West to me,
  With its loud sea-lashings,
  And cliff-side clashings
Of waters rife with revelry.

She opened the door of Romance to me,
  The door from a cell
  I had known too well,
Too long, till then, and was fain to flee.

She opened the door of a Love to me,
  That passed the wry
  World-welters by
As far as the arching blue the lea.

She opens the door of the Past to me,
  Its magic lights,
  Its heavenly heights,
When forward little is to see!

1913

133

After the Visit

(To F.E.D.)

COME again to the place
Where your presence was as a leaf that skims
Down a drouthy way whose ascent bedims
The bloom on the farer's face.

Come again, with the feet
That were light on the green as a thistledown ball,
And those mute ministrations to one and to all
Beyond a man's saying sweet.

Until then the faint scent
Of the bordering flowers swam unheeded away,
And I marked not the charm in the changes of day
As the cloud-colours came and went.

Through the dark corridors
Your walk was so soundless I did not know
Your form from a phantom's of long ago
Said to pass on the ancient floors,

Till you drew from the shade,
And I saw the large luminous living eyes
Regard me in fixed inquiring-wise
As those of a soul that weighed,

Scarce consciously,
The eternal question of what Life was,
And why we were there, and by whose strange laws
That which mattered most could not be.

I Sometimes Think

(For F.E.H.)

I SOMETIMES think as here I sit
   Of things I have done,
Which seemed in doing not unfit
   To face the sun:
Yet never a soul has paused a whit
   On such–not one.

There was that eager strenuous press
   To sow good seed;
There was that saving from distress
   In the nick of need;
There were those words in the wilderness:
   Who cared to heed?

Yet can this be full true, or no?
   For one did care,
And, spiriting into my house, to, fro,
   Like wind on the stair,
Cares still, heeds all, and will, even though
   I may despair.

In Time of
'The Breaking of Nations'

ONLY a man harrowing clods
    In a slow silent walk
With an old horse that stumbles and nods
    Half asleep as they stalk.

Only thin smoke without flame
    From the heaps of couch-grass;
Yet this will go onward the same
    Though Dynasties pass.

Yonder a maid and her wight
    Come whispering by:
War's annals will cloud into night
    Ere their story die.

1915

Drummer Hodge

THEY throw in Drummer Hodge, to rest
    Uncoffined—just as found:
His landmark is a kopje-crest
    That breaks the veldt around;
And foreign constellations west
    Each night above his mound.

Young Hodge the Drummer never knew—
    Fresh from his Wessex home—
The meaning of the broad Karoo,
    The Bush, the dusty loam,
And why uprose to nightly view
    Strange stars amid the gloam.

Yet portion of that unknown plain
    Will Hodge for ever be;
His homely Northern breast and brain
    Grow to some Southern tree,
And strange-eyed constellations reign
    His stars eternally.

His Country

He travels southward, and looks around;

I JOURNEYED from my native spot
 Across the south sea shine,
And found that people in hall and cot
Laboured and suffered each his lot
 Even as I did mine.

and cannot discover the boundary

Thus noting them in meads and marts
 It did not seem to me
That my dear country with its hearts,
Minds, yearnings, worse and better parts
 Had ended with the sea.

of his native country;

I further and further went anon,
 As such I still surveyed,
And further yet—yea, on and on,
And all the men I looked upon
 Had heart-strings fellow-made.

I traced the whole terrestrial round,
  Homing the other side;
Then said I, 'What is there to bound
My denizenship? It seems I have found
  Its scope to be world-wide.'

or where
his duties to
his fellow-
creatures end;

I asked me: 'Whom have I to fight,
  And whom have I to dare,
And whom to weaken, crush, and blight?
My country seems to have kept in sight
  On my way everywhere.'

nor who are
his enemies.

1913

Men Who March Away

(Song of the Soldiers)

WHAT of the faith and fire within us
Men who march away,
Ere the barn-cocks say
Night is growing gray,
Leaving all that here can win us;
What of the faith and fire within us
Men who march away?

Is it a purblind prank, O think you,
Friend with the musing eye,
Who watch us stepping by
With doubt and dolorous sigh?
Can much pondering so hoodwink you!
Is it a purblind prank, O think you,
Friend with the musing eye?

Nay. We well see what we are doing,
Though some may not see—
Dalliers as they be—
England's need are we;
Her distress would leave us ruing:
Nay. We well see what we are doing,
Though some may not see!

In our heart of hearts believing
Victory crowns the just,
And that braggarts must
Surely bite the dust,
Press we to the field ungrieving,
In our heart of hearts believing
Victory crowns the just.

Before Marching and After

(In Memoriam F.W.G.)

ORION swung southward aslant
Where the starved Egdon pine-trees had thinned,
The Pleiads aloft seemed to pant
With the heather that twitched in the wind;
But he looked on indifferent to sights such as these,
Unswayed by love, friendship, home joy or home sorrow,
And wondered to what he would march on the morrow.

The crazed household-clock with its whirr
Rang midnight within as he stood,
He heard the low sighing of her
Who had striven from his birth for his good;
But he still only asked the spring starlight, the breeze,
What great thing or small thing his history would borrow
From that Game with Death he would play on the morrow.

When the heath wore the robe of late summer,
And the fuchsia-bells, hot in the sun,
Hung red by the door, a quick comer
Brought tidings that marching was done
For him who had joined in that game overseas
Where Death stood to win, though his name was to borrow
A brightness therefrom not to fade on the morrow.

September 1915

'And There Was a Great Calm'

(On the Signing of the Armistice, 11 Nov. 1918)

THERE had been years of Passion—scorching, cold,
And much Despair, and Anger heaving high,
Care whitely watching, Sorrows manifold,
Among the young, among the weak and old,
And the pensive Spirit of Pity whispered, 'Why?'

Men had not paused to answer. Foes distraught
Pierced the thinned peoples in a brute-like blindness,
Philosophies that sages long had taught,
And Selflessness, were as an unknown thought,
And 'Hell!' and 'Shell!' were yapped at Lovingkindness.

The feeble folk at home had grown full-used
To 'dug-outs', 'snipers', 'Huns', from the war-adept
In the morning's heard, and at evetides perused;
To day-dreamt men in millions, when they mused—
To nightmare-men in millions when they slept.

Waking to wish existence timeless, null,
Sirius they watched above where armies fell;
He seemed to check his flapping when, in the lull
Of night a boom came thencewise, like the dull
Plunge of a stone dropped into some deep well.

So, when old hopes that earth was bettering slowly
Were dead and damned, there sounded 'War is done!'
One morrow. Said the bereft, and meek, and lowly,
'Will men some day be given to grace? yea, wholly,
And in good sooth, as our dreams used to run?'

Breathless they paused. Out there men raised their glance
To where had stood those poplars lank and lopped,
As they had raised it through the four years' dance
Of Death in the now familiar flats of France;
And murmured, 'Strange, this! How? All firing stopped?'

Aye; all was hushed. The about-to-fire fired not,
The aimed-at moved away in trance-lipped song.
One checkless regiment slung a clinching shot
And turned. The Spirit of Irony smirked out, 'What?
Spoil peradventures woven of Rage and Wrong?'

Thenceforth no flying fires inflamed the gray,
No hurtlings shook the dewdrop from the thorn,
No moan perplexed the mute bird on the spray;
Worn horses mused: 'We are not whipped to-day;'
No weft-winged engines blurred the moon's thin horn.

Calm fell. From Heaven distilled a clemency;
There was peace on earth, and silence in the sky;
Some could, some could not, shake off misery:
The Sinister Spirit sneered: 'It had to be!'
And again the Spirit of Pity whispered, 'Why?'

Memory and I

'O MEMORY, where is now my youth,
Who used to say that life was truth?'

'I saw him in a crumbled cot
    Beneath a tottering tree;
That he as phantom lingers there
    Is only known to me.'

'O Memory, where is now my joy,
Who lived with me in sweet employ?'

'I saw him in gaunt gardens lone,
    Where laughter used to be;
That he as phantom wanders there
    Is known to none but me.'

'O Memory, where is now my hope,
Who charged with deeds my skill and scope?'

'I saw her in a tomb of tomes,
    Where dreams are wont to be;
That she as spectre haunteth there
    Is only known to me'.

'O Memory, where is now my faith,
One time a champion, now a wraith?'

'I saw her in a ravaged aisle,
    Bowed down on bended knee;
That her poor ghost outflickers there
    Is known to none but me'.

'O Memory, where is now my love,
That rayed me as a god above?'

'I saw her in an ageing shape
    Where beauty used to be;
That her fond phantom lingers there
    Is only known to me'.

Afterwards

WHEN the Present has latched its postern behind my tremulous stay,
    And the May month flaps its glad green leaves like wings,
Delicate-filmed as new-spun silk, will the neighbours say,
    'He was a man who used to notice such things'?

If it be in the dusk when, like an eyelid's soundless blink,
    The dewfall-hawk comes crossing the shades to alight
Upon the wind-warped upland thorn, a gazer may think,
    'To him this must have been a familiar sight'.

If I pass during some nocturnal blackness, mothy and warm,
    When the hedgehog travels furtively over the lawn,
One may say, 'He strove that such innocent creatures should come
        to no harm,
    But he could do little for them; and now he is gone'.

If, when hearing that I have been stilled at last, they stand at the door,
    Watching the full-starred heavens that winter sees,
Will this thought rise on those who will meet my face no more,
    'He was one who had an eye for such mysteries'?

And will any say when my bell of quittance is heard in the gloom,
    And a crossing breeze cuts a pause in its outrollings,
Till they rise again, as they were a new bell's boom,
    'He hears it not now, but used to notice such things'?

He Never Expected Much

(or)
A consideration
(A reflection) on My Eighty-Sixth Birthday

WELL, World, you have kept faith with me
      Kept faith with me;
Upon the whole you have proved to be
      Much as you said you were.
Since as a child I used to lie
Upon the leaze and watch the sky,
Never, I own, expected I
      That life would all be fair.

'Twas then you said, and since have said,
      Times since have said,
In that mysterious voice you shed
      From clouds and hills around:
'Many have loved me desperately,
Many with smooth serenity,
While some have shown contempt of me
      Till they dropped underground.

'I do not promise overmuch,
Child; overmuch;
Just neutral-tinted haps and such',
You said to minds like mine.
Wise warning for your credit's sake!
Which I for one failed not to take,
And hence could stem such strain and ache
As each year might assign.

So Various

YOU may have met a man – quite young –
A brisk-eyed youth, and highly strung;
  One whose desires
  And inner fires
  Moved him as wires.

And you may have met one stiff and old,
If not in years; of manner cold;
  Who seemed as stone,
  And never had known
  Of mirth or moan.

And there may have crossed your path a lover,
In whose clear depths you could discover
  A staunch, robust,
  And tender trust,
  Through storm and gust.

And you may have also known one fickle,
Whose fancies changed as the silver sickle
  Of yonder moon,
  Which shapes soon
  To demilune!

You entertained a person once
Whom you internally deemed a dunce:—
    As he sat in view
    Just facing you
    You saw him through.

You came to know a learned seer
Of whom you read the surface mere:
    Your soul quite sank;
    Brain of such rank
    Dubbed yours a blank.

Anon you quizzed a man of sadness,
Who never could have known true gladness:
    Just for a whim
    You pitied him
    In his sore trim.

You journeyed with a man so glad
You never could conceive him sad:
    He proved to be
    Indubitably
    Good company.

You lit on an unadventurous slow man,
Who, said you, need be feared by no man;

That his slack deeds
And sloth must needs
Produce but weeds.

A man of enterprise, shrewd and swift,
Who never suffered affairs to drift,
You eyed for a time
Just in his prime,
And judged he might climb.

You smoked beside one who forgot
All that you said, or grasped it not.
Quite a poor thing
Not worth a sting
By satirizing!

Next year you nearly lost for ever
Goodwill from one who forgot slights never;
And, with unease,
Felt you must seize
Occasion to please....

Now.... All these specimens of man,
So various in their pith and plan,
Curious to say
Were one man. Yea,
I was all they.

He Resolves to Say No More

O MY soul, keep the rest unknown!
It is too like a sound of moan
    When the charnel-eyed
    Pale Horse has nighed:
Yea, none shall gather what I hide!

Why load men's minds with more to bear
That bear already ails to spare?
    From now alway,
    Till my last day,
What I discern I will not say.

Let Time roll backward if it will;
(Magians who drive the midnight quill
    With brain aglow
    Can see it so,)
What I have learnt no man shall know.

And if my vision range beyond
The blinkered sight of souls in bond,
    —By truth made free—
    I'll let all be,
And show to no man what I see.

Surview

A CRY from the green-grained sticks of the fire
    Made me gaze where it seemed to be:
'Twas my own voice talking therefrom to me
On how I had walked when my sun was higher—
    My heart in its arrogancy.

'You held not to whatsover was true,'
    Said my own voice talking to me:
'Whatsover was just you were slack to see;
Kept not things lovely and pure in view,'
    Said my own voice talking to me.

'You slighted her that endureth all,'
    Said my own voice talking to me;
'Vaunteth not, trusteth hopefully;
That suffereth long and is kind withal,'
    Said my own voice talking to me.

'You taught not that which you set about,'
    Said my own voice talking to me;
'That the greatest of things is Charity....'
—And the sticks burnt low, and the fire went out,
    And my voice ceased talking to me.